POMPEII
THE LOST CITY

Contents

D0530861

Written by Fiona Macdonald

Illustrated by Giorgio Bacchin

A fine city

Pompeii was a city in Italy. It was built in ancient Roman times, about 2,000 years ago.

Italy

Vesuvius

Pompeii

A huge mountain, called Vesuvius, towered over Pompeii. Today, we know that Vesuvius is a **volcano**.

Pompeii

Vesuvius

3

Pompeii was big and busy – about 20,000 people lived there. They came from Italy, Greece and Africa, and they worked as **traders** and sailors.

5

Volcano danger

Vesuvius began to **erupt** in AD 79.
A mighty earthquake shook
the ground. Clouds of ash hid
the sun and the sky went dark.
The people of Pompeii were terrified.

The eruption lasted for two days.
A massive explosion hurled rocks
into the sky. Red-hot **lava**
poured out of
the volcano.

*Lava came from deep
beneath the earth's surface.*

Deadly clouds of burning gas rolled over Pompeii. The air was full of falling ash, which looked like black snow.

Vesuvius erupting, hurling rocks and ash into the sky

No escape!

Everyone in Pompeii tried to escape, but the roads were blocked with lava, ash and mud. At sea, strong winds caused by the heat of the volcano pushed ships back to the shore.

9

Dead and buried

Thousands of people in Pompeii were killed.
Most were burnt alive. Others died after
breathing dust or poisonous gas.

Ash from Vesuvius fell for two days and it covered all of Pompeii. The whole city disappeared.

Slowly, over hundreds of years, the layers of ash stuck together and turned into rock. Pompeii's buildings, carvings, coins, cooking pots, paintings, **mosaics** and statues were **preserved** inside the rock. But the bodies of people and animals rotted away.

For hundreds of years, no-one knew that the ruins of Pompeii were buried under the ground.

Finding the lost city

For the past 400 years, people have been digging into the rock around Pompeii. They have discovered buildings, paintings and many other things from Roman times.

Here are some of the things that the diggers found. They show us what life was like in Pompeii long ago.

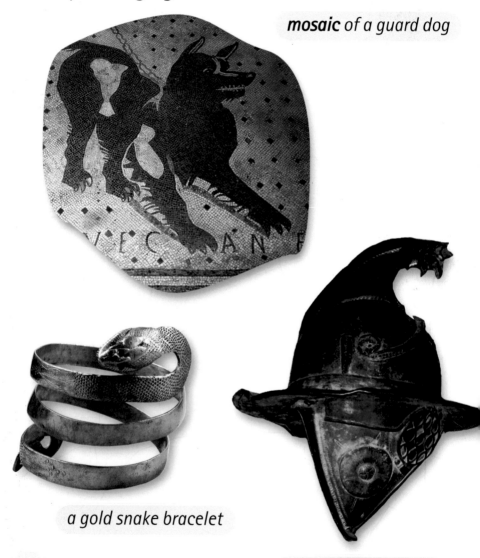

mosaic of a guard dog

a gold snake bracelet

a gladiator's helmet

ruins of a shop that sold take-away food

Pompeii today

Today, Pompeii is world-famous – over two million people go there every year. They walk along Roman streets and look inside Roman shops and houses. They learn what life was like 2,000 years ago. Going to Pompeii is like travelling back in time!

Glossary

erupt   when a volcano becomes active and throws out lava, gases and ash

gladiator   a man in Roman times trained to fight against other men or wild animals for entertainment

lava   hot liquid rock that erupts from volcanoes

mosaic   pictures made of small pieces of pottery or stone

preserved   kept safe from danger or harm

traders   people who buy and sell goods

volcano   a mountain that can erupt, throwing out lava and ash

Index

Pompeii – a timeline

Vesuvius exploded, AD 79

AD 12   500   100

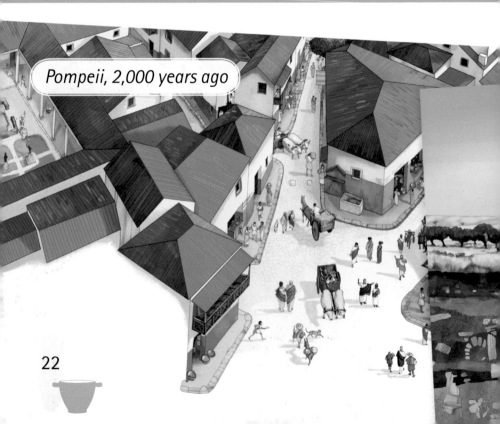

Pompeii, 2,000 years ago

Pompeii uncovered, 1600s

1500   2000

Pompeii today

Pompeii underground

⁛ Ideas for reading ⁛

Written by Clare Dowdall BA(Ed), MA(Ed)
Lecturer and Primary Literacy Consultant

Learning objectives: know how to tackle unfamiliar words that are not completely decodable; draw together ideas and information from across a whole text, using simple signposts in the text; give some reasons why things happen; explain ideas and processes using imaginative and adventurous vocabulary; adopt appropriate roles in small or large groups and consider alternative courses of action

Curriculum links: History; Geography

Interest words: Pompeii, buried, Vesuvius, poisonous, erupt, lava, mosaics, preserved, traders, volcano

Word count: 333

Resources: interest and glossary words on flashcards, internet

Getting started

- Look at the front cover of the book and ask children to describe what they can see in the illustration. Discuss what a volcano is and what happens when one explodes.

- Explain that this is an information book that will describe what happened when a volcano called Vesuvius exploded near the Ancient Roman city of Pompeii. Ask children if they have heard of Pompeii, and ask them to suggest what may have happened to it.

- Introduce the interest and glossary words to children using flashcards. Help the children to read the words using phonics skills and strategies where appropriate, e.g. *p-oi-s-o-n-ou-s*.

Reading and responding

- Look at pp2–3 together. Read the text and help children to understand that the city of Pompeii is 2,000 years old. Orientate children to the map, and help them to relate the photograph on p3 with the map on p2 by drawing their attention to the labels.

- Model how to read for information using pp4–5. Talk aloud as you describe what you can see in the images, e.g. *the gardens look beautiful.*